We Meant to
BRING IT HOME
Alive

We Meant to BRING IT HOME Alive

POEMS
Armin Tolentino

Alternating Current Press
Boulder, Colorado

We Meant to Bring It Home Alive
Armin Tolentino
©2019 Alternating Current Press

Alternating Current
Boulder, Colorado
alternatingcurrentarts.com

ISBN-10: 1-946580-07-4
ISBN-13: 978-1-946580-07-8
First Edition: March 2019

ADVANCE PRAISE

"It's a daunting task to find empathy for the incredible, but in Armin Tolentino's *We Meant to Bring It Home Alive*, he is able to shift from the connective tissue of emotion and loss to the outlandish landscapes of space and earthly adventures. As he would put it: 'frozen oceans, buried cities, graves / and all that distance' are all images that can live within the individual if that individual can take a deep-enough breath. This collection shakes off the traditional containment poetry can struggle against and lives wildly with each wing flap of a dragon and each disappearance of the sun. With such fullness, Tolentino managed to surprise me over and over again by quickly removing these dynamic images, and leaving the speaker in the poem to say, 'Or / no more.' You don't expect work with such a fantastic energy to find an almost equally haunting quality, but that's what happens when you experience the full range of these poems."

—**Darren C. Demaree**,
author of *Emily As Sometimes the Forest Wants the Fire*

"Armin Tolentino's poems reach across time and space, Biblical in scope, longing, and wonder. These poems ask us to consider how we map a way back to each other and to the unknown. There's no shortage of miracles here: dragons, spaceboys, angel meat, and lizard fights, yet extinction waits at every turn. Here is a poet who writes with the fever of time running out: 'The Lord Almighty is just, / His message clear, and the wise man's heart can tell (minus or plus / a day) eclipses and earthquakes are near; it must / buy billboard space and warn the less discerning.' Perhaps we should listen."

—**Ruth Awad**,
author of *Set to Music a Wildfire*

"Brimming with imagination and melody, *We Meant to Bring It Home Alive* is a spooky deep-dive through the intersections of myth, spirituality, and Americana."

—**Deb Jannerson**,
author of *Rabbit Rabbit* and *Thanks for Nothing*

"Daring and awe battle hubris and cowardice throughout the hypnotic rhythms and kaleidoscopic motifs of *We Meant to Bring It Home Alive*. Delving into deep space, deep earth, and human folly, Armin Tolentino evokes the likes of *Moby Dick*, 'Space Oddity,' Commander Keen, Genesis, and the Gospels. Unreceived letters and black box recordings seem to converse, impossibly, across empty darkness; 'the liturgy of numbers' offers hope to a wife on a widow's walk, while numerology entices a radio preacher; an astronaut returns to Earth after years of deep-space hibernation to witness the aftermath of mass extinction beneath a dying sun; longing and absence fill the space of a rapidly expanding universe. Meanwhile, on Earth, mankind gambles with God and the angels, and the game isn't yet over—who will and won't see whose hands? *We Meant to Bring It Home Alive* barrels out to the horizons of knowing, to 'stand / on the thin division between *is* and *is not*,' elegantly questioning humanity's relationship to our planet's past and increasingly uncertain future. Mesmerizing, thought-provoking, and deliciously entertaining, Tolentino's collection will haunt your dreams."

—**Allison Boyd Justus**,
author of *Solstice to Solstice to Solstice*

"The mesmerizing wonder captured in Tolentino's poems evokes both confrontation and longing. Through the incredible, he pulls out some of the rawest emotions of human existence: awe, isolation, ache. Space travel might not be available to all quite yet, but Tolentino's poems are the closest experience to floating, fascinated among the stars, as we can get."

—**Đỗ Nguyên Mai**,
author of *Ghosts Still Walking*

TABLE OF CONTENTS

Welcome Home, Spaceboy!

Dragon Scrimshaw · 17
Spaceboy's First Mission, Age Twelve · 18
A Letter That Spaceboy Never Received · 20
Spaceboy's Wife Builds a Widow's Walk · 22
Spaceboy Gives a Eulogy at His Mentor's Funeral · 23
Black Box Recording · 24
Suspended Memories · 25
Last Words for an Evening Vigil · 26
A Letter That Spaceboy Never Received · 27
Stress Tests and Survival Skills · 28
A Letter That Spaceboy Never Received · 29
Black Box Recording · 30
Falling Sky, Hope Smoldering · 31
A Letter That Spaceboy Never Received · 32
Last Words for an Evening Vigil · 33
A Letter That Spaceboy Never Received · 34
Black Box Recording · 35
A Letter That Spaceboy Never Received · 36
Last Words for an Evening Vigil · 37
A Letter That Spaceboy Never Received · 38
Spaceboy's First Mission, Age Twelve · 39
Welcome Home, Spaceboy! · 40
Adrift at Sea Beneath the Dragon's Watch · 41

A Week's Pay Lost at the Lizard Fight

Within the Bird Storm · 49
The EPA Warns Against Consumption of Angel Meat · 50
A Week's Pay Lost at the Lizard Fight · 51
Caterpillars · 52
Origins of the Lizard Man · 53
In the Dunkin' Donuts Where the Virgin Mary Appeared on an Apple
    Fritter · 54
The Northernmost Edge of the Star-Wasting Syndrome · 55
Anton LaVey's Blazer · 56
Standing Naked in the Forest at the Height of Mosquito Season · 57
Dirt Eaters Anonymous · 58
The Gospel According to *Homo Habilis* · 59

The Hard Hand of Cataclysm

In Mission, Kansas, on the Brink of the Latest Apocalypse · 67
"Fear not for I am with thee," · 68
A Refugee of the Bone Wars · 69
Gambler's Ruin, Blue Stag Casino · 71
Field of Bullets, Medicine Bow · 72
"He that is without sin among you, let him first cast a stone." · 73
A Reading from the Book of Modern Extinctions · 74
"... a wise man's heart discerneth both time and judgment." · 77
Simple Math, Sweet Grass County · 78
"For He shall give His angels charge over you and keep you in all your
      ways," · 80
The Second Pass of the Scythe · 81
"And He arose, and rebuked the wind, and said unto the sea, Peace, be
      still." · 83
Complex Math, Teton County · 84
Growing Old in the Ribcage of Extinction · 85
Minimum Viable Population, Cape Alava · 88
"Unto Adam also and to his wife did the LORD God make coats of skins,
      and clothed them." · 90

Matter

Advance Praise · 5
About the Author · 95
Author Notes on the Text · 96
Author Thanks · 98
Acknowledgments · 99
Colophon · 100

For *Jenny*

I always find my way back to you.

We Meant to
BRING IT HOME
Alive

Welcome HOME, Spaceboy!

"I write to remember
'Cause I'm a million miles away
Will you get this letter?"

—*At the Drive-In, "One Armed Scissor"*

DRAGON SCRIMSHAW

We meant to bring it home alive, the dragon
 we found writhing on the ice fields of the Arctic Sea,
stranded by its shattered wing. Fixed its helpless weight
to the ship's side and offered it our rationed meat.
Try as we did to rinse its yellow eyes of salt,
still it died. One harpooner plucked a tooth to scrimshaw.

Captain found out about the thieving scrimshander,
lashed his legs seven times screaming that a dead dragon
was still worth more than a thousand barrels of oil; the salt
would preserve it. But we begged to cut it loose, let it sink into the sea.
Too heavy to tow and sharks were nipping chunks of meat
from its belly. But Captain said the corpse would pay its weight

in gold. We sailed a slow route home, the extra weight
a burden. Without whaling, killed time with smoke and scrimshaw,
dreamt of women soaked in syrup and wine who would meet
us at port. In spring, we crossed Cancer and skies erupted as if the dragon
had breathed its doomed flames into the thunderclaps. The sea
churned black beneath us. The storm waged an assault,

the deck punished with rain until each man was swallowed by salt
water or stabbed by screws of lightning. Except me. The weight
of the first mate's body sheltered me until the heartbeat of the sea
slowed to near stillness. I drifted alone and scrimshawed
my daughter's name on teeth I pulled from the mouth of the dragon
to count each passing day. By thirty thousand, I'd run out of meat,

hardtack, and cod. I sliced the creature's back, cubes of scaly meat
I dried on the deck, old gray flesh packed hard with salt.
When, one day, I saw the sun eclipsed by a swarm of dragons,
I knew I'd never see my home again. The weight
of their shadows smothered me as they crossed heaven. I scrimshawed
my questions to God on vertebrae as I drifted a borderless sea.

I've tossed out the spyglass because I know what I'll see:
blue on blue horizon, where sky and water meet.
I've burned the sails for soot to color my scrimshaw;
I never seem to run out of bones. I drink buckets of salt
water, but I never seem to run out of life. I wait
for nothing, and nothing comes, as the centuries drag on.

SPACEBOY'S FIRST MISSION, AGE TWELVE

A dozen poplar logs, dried and light
as Styrofoam, dragged from the forest
and fastened with jute
we snuck from Dad's toolbox.
Summer vacation testing buoyancy
on the lake from whose center
an island bloomed,
glittering alien planet,
and no way to know
how many fathoms we'd sink
if our knots should relax
or the wood suck too much water.

The night before our launch,
I asked, *What do you think
we'll find?*
He was packing provisions:
fishhooks, compass, chocolate chip cookies,
a book mapping stars.

*Mammoth bones or ruins,
probably,* he shrugged.
*Just hope we don't see
any dragons. Whalers used to say,*

*A dragon at sea meant you'd never
make it back home.*

Next morning, I faked sickness
and confessed to our parents
the summer-long project
when he didn't come home by dinner.
Dad borrowed a neighbor's skiff
and my brother was grounded,
telescope privileges forbidden, as well.

He wouldn't even look at me.
*At least you didn't see
a dragon,* I said.

He stared out the window.
It was dark too soon already.
His anger, my gratitude—
two stars to navigate us to the equinox.

His words fogged the window.
How do you know I didn't?

A Letter That Spaceboy Never Received

*Y*ou wouldn't know, at T-minus 7
I shut my eyes
from the shuttle's exhaust,

a blossom of orange that burned itself
into gray. Couldn't shake the feeling
you'd just strapped yourself

inside the throat of a dragon.
The crowd sang goodbye,
at zero you broke the thick quilt

of cumulus, but
I never watched you go.
Another confession:

The summer we built a log raft
with twine, a handbook on knots,
and no knowledge of nautical physics,

I wasn't too sick to join in the journey,
just a copilot frozen by the unshakeable thought
the lake was alive and halfway across

would love us too much to ever
let us go. If I sank, what would Mom have
to lay in my coffin? Would my soul snap loose

from its anchor of bones?
How would it find the surface?
That morning you sailed,

offered her prow
to the water's give, but I witnessed
nothing, locked in the bathroom,

crying too much to wish you
good luck.

Since blastoff, I've trained my eyes
to stay open, to stare at stretches of sky

without tiring, so patient I now can spot
black migrations of midges against empty
miles of blue. Brother, I promise I will not blink,

I will not flinch, pull back this time,
I will not miss one second of your return.

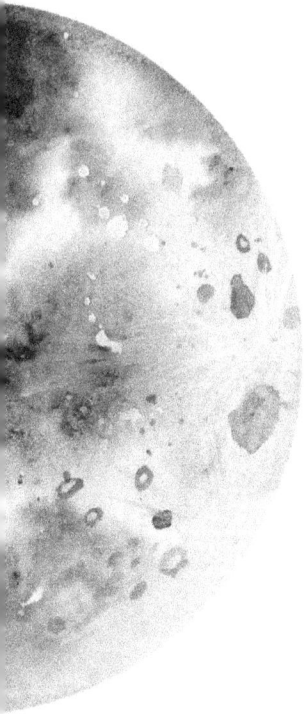

Spaceboy's Wife Builds a Widow's Walk

*I*t's not as if she doesn't yearn
to know as much as he,

to distill darkness and distance
into a single equation,

both Newton and quantum
secure in her fingers,

two halves of a lover's heart
she aches to sew an equal sign through.

It's just—
she doesn't need to *touch* it.

She believes in
the liturgy of numbers.

Strings of digits stretched across
a college blackboard:

a tabernacle for the sacrament of
unquestionable truth.

Not him. Doubting Thomas
will believe only if his fingers sink

into black holes. At liftoff,
she wept, a cloudy day that blurred

as the shuttle shrank to microscopic.
He left her nothing but a question

theoretical physics couldn't answer.
Spaceboy's wife builds a widow's walk

to perform her first experiment:
how many steps back and forth across

a twelve-foot span of roof will elapse before
his shuttle flukes the atmosphere again?

Too many variables to reduce and she fears
for this equation absence is the constant.

Spaceboy Gives a Eulogy at His Mentor's Funeral

How could your story   end this way,

hollowed and buried   in Bayonne,

New Jersey?   We should have returned

your body to stardust,

dressed you with incense   and garlanded fireworks over your chest

to jettison you into sparkling darkness,

most distant shore of the sky,   where you could explode

into supernova and fall back

to Earth some future day

when we would most need

a reminder

of your light.

We should have split

your ribcage open   and offered the splayed

red halves to heaven.

BLACK BOX
RECORDING

*F*lickers
of doubt flared up.
At liftoff, I cried *I'm
sorry*. I just couldn't live with
what if.

Suspended Memories

"I think my spaceship knows which way to go.
Tell my wife I love her very much.
She knows."

A chip shuts off the nerves that wire my brain.
Synapses hushed to begin hibernation.
My winter sleep and silence lasts an Earth year.
But in this coma, buried in the gray,
memory still hums. I wake with a name
on my tongue—but can't recall who she is.

Reanimation lasts barely an hour,
just long enough to send a transmission:
coordinates and confirmation of life.
Nothing to say, nothing to steer. Nothing
to worry about—after all, *she knows*—but
I'm losing her name as I sink once again in the sea
of my sleep. On the surface, a memory floats
distorted by currents. I hold my breath
and flail for it until, exhausted, I surrender.
The lights in my skull blink off one by one.

A handful of neurons left buzzing, I fight
the chip, sit up, fumble a name that haunts me,
accuse the darkness: Who are you?
What do you know? Do you remember
my name? Did you once love me? Are you hiding
in this darkness? The ship alone responds.
She tells me to sleep. It's a long ride. *Just sleep*.

LAST WORDS
FOR AN EVENING VIGIL

W hat if
    each night I light
enough candles, they fuse
the knot of a new North Star you'd
follow?

A Letter That Spaceboy Never Received

*D*o you remember Mom making us
 tea on snow days? You never took honey,
but savored the bitterness,

thinking things that adults forbade
were always acrid—coffee, whiskey, smoke—
like you were reaching for the future

in a cup of biting darkness. Back then
you guessed the universe was shaped
like a teacup, dipping in the center

with all the matter that had ever existed
floating in its walls. You had no proof,
but still I pestered: If I could somehow run

fast enough against the curve, and climb
that slope, could I reach the lip and stand
on the thin division between *is* and *is not*

and if so, would I feel wind?
Do you know the answer now?

STRESS TESTS
AND SURVIVAL SKILLS

Light deprivation, twelve days
bound in shrouds of black
plastic. I breathed through
tubes. Streams of fluid
pumped into my wrist. I learned
the sound liquid makes
as it works through the body's
waterways. Nothing to do
but listen and breathe in a replica
of the galaxy's borders, a darkness where
the fingers of stars
can never reach. I didn't open
my eyes—not once—to prove
there was nothing missing,
nothing more I needed than
the rhythm of my body surviving.
       Then, I was released,
unhooked and dizzy. Without a break
or bite of solid food, they moved me
to a sterile room, so white I kept
my eyes shut until the burning lessened.
There, a book on origami,
a stack of plain white paper. A single
command through loudspeakers:
Fold one thousand cranes.
Just another test of endurance
and I folded the layers, crease over
crease, until the paper blistered
my fingers with dry friction.
       Now, with the shuttle's engines
shattered, I understand it wasn't testing,
but training, and I've folded ten thousand
cranes that float about the capsule, one
for every lightyear I've drifted away
from Earth.

A Letter That Spaceboy Never Received

*I*n place of a best man
I kept in my pocket the meteorite
you gave me for graduation,

a shocking weight, made of space's
densest metals. You explained how
falling stars splintered from the same

extinct planet, leaving its ruins between
Mars and Jupiter, a belt of broken continents
haunting the sun, and perhaps now I carried

the frozen core of a dead world in my jacket,
all that was left when the atmosphere
shaved off its burning layers. It sagged

my tux in the photos. My mother-in-law
complained, but that's what I wanted,
for us always to have proof you were there.

Black Box
Recording

*F*ollow
Andromeda
south. See me waving? A
galaxy away, I still hear
your voice.

Falling Sky, Hope Smoldering

*I*nitial reports claim a white scar
streaking the desert sky, sonic boom
and wind, broken glass in Vegas over

300 miles away, a shockwave so sudden
gamblers drop their drinks and remorseful
addicts repent on Flamingo Ave. Star-

watcher websites crash from the volume
of amateur photos, a crater
punishing the wastelands of Sonora, smoking

chunk of sky in the center. NASA reps dispel
rumors of alien convoys, Korean ballistics, or
the extinction of man. Just a satellite blown

off course—of course—but Spaceboy's
wife is there when they pry open
the burned metal, each of them stunned

by a hiss of oxygen, the fuselage frigid,
years untouched by starlight.
Dashboard instruments blink feebly, a capsule

predating microchips, fashioned with slide rules
and pencils. Strapped in the passenger's seat,
she touches America's first astronaut,

a Rhesus monkey, circa 1952,
skinny, frozen,
but still breathing.

A Letter That Spaceboy Never Received

*Y*our nephew did a project
   on his hero, Uncle Spaceboy,
the keeper of stars, he who stared

down the eye of Jupiter without
flinching. He tells his classmates,

Someday, I'll meet him
and he'll let me fly the spaceship.

At night he listens for your landing.
He asked to strap my letters
on fireworks so the ashes

would lead you back to us—
in case you'd forgotten your way—
a breadcrumb trail back home.

Last Words
for an Evening Vigil

*Y*our voice
redshifts as you
leave me further behind.
That is, my memory of you is
stretched, faint.

A Letter That Spaceboy Never Received

The divorce was finalized and neither of us
won anything but silent evenings once the world

falls asleep. When the insomnia gets unbearable
I scan radio static, hoping to hear accidental

transmissions, love songs from distant planets.
You are moving so quickly through the darkness

that you must not be aging, stripping cords of time
that tangle us down here. You may not recognize me.

Gravity pulls my skin loose, the creases
caked with dust.

Black Box
Recording

*S*tretched. Faint
thirst. Awoke to
another decade dead,
thinking you must be so old. Or
no more.

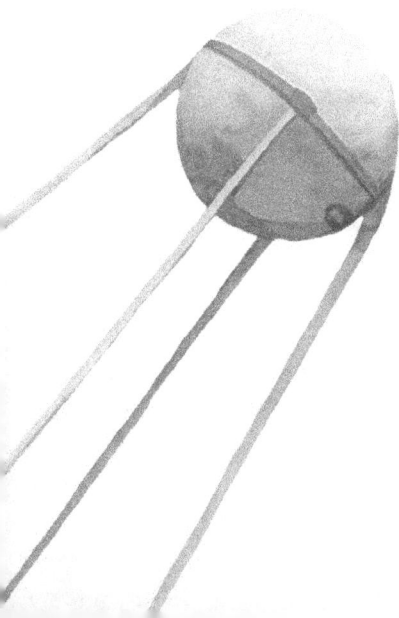

A Letter That Spaceboy
Never Received

*D*ad died.
  He asked to be cremated
hoping the smoke would reach you
for a proper goodbye.

LAST WORDS
FOR AN EVENING VIGIL

No more
candles. I used
to light the house on fire.
My hope emitted heat. Now I barely
flicker.

A Letter That Spaceboy Never Received

*I*f you return in time, let's sit on the porch
 on a slow-motion Sunday, nursing cold beer
and afternoon sun, so you can tell me

what you've learned all these years,
what heaven taught you, how close
to the periphery you let your fingers wander.

And before the mosquitoes come to feast
on the blood that sours inside this old man,
let me share what I've learned while you've

been away: deep earth preserves the bones
of angels who'd grown too weak
to break through the atmosphere.

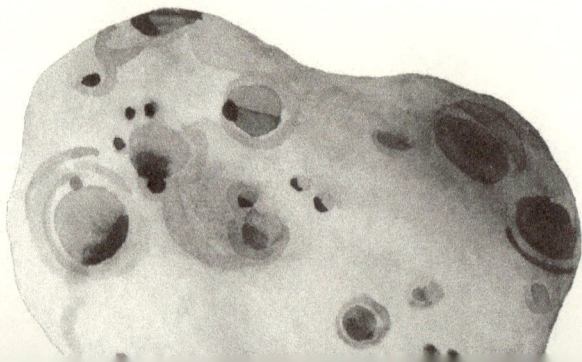

Spaceboy's First Mission, Age Twelve

The *what-ifs* storm the deck of his thoughts.

He lost the paddle and, like the raft, has lost
control over his fear.

              Gale winds of regret
churn up the sobs that surge his chest.
        He's exhausted.

He drifts into dusk with no do-overs.
Wishes he'd packed a coat.
        Already shivering, the starry
night won't forgive him.   Wishes most

he'd left a letter.
        I loved you all. I'm really,
               really sorry.

That great ship, the Sun, is capsized by darkness,

but, free of its glare, he's awed
                how close he came
to the island of his longing.   Its trees
in full night have erupted with tiny yellow flames.

Likely lightning bugs. Or perhaps
        many thousand dragons' eyes
watching what he'll do next.

        He holds his breath and dives.

WELCOME HOME, SPACEBOY!

Long ago the banners fell,
bleached, then rotted,
        waiting his homecoming.

The world he left
        is now sealed between layers of faded eras

        like leaves pressed and dried
                from the fall of a girl's first kiss.

Spaceboy skids the surface of Earth
        waxing in its final phase:

        Epoch of Exhausted Sun,

where the creatures that survived
              make do beneath
        a pale pink flicker
              that's lost her children,
no longer the center of anything.

        On this drifting planet,
shocked by the weight of his flesh,

he mouths the countdown, overjoyed,
        T-minus his fading pulse

woozy on the deck   of another lost ship
        as he's pulled by the urge
              of shale and mantle,
frozen oceans, buried cities, graves,
        and all that distance
              he still could never bridge.

ADRIFT AT SEA BENEATH THE DRAGON'S WATCH

*Draco, the dragon constellation, is circumpolar; it never sets
in the northern latitudes and is visible every night of the year.*

Seal my mouth with paraffin,
        I've nothing left to say.
                No psalm, no chantey, no curse,
        no confession. I've stripped
                my throat raw screaming rescue,
but the sea has replied the same:
                There is no home for you.

                If Earth were flat,
        I'd float off the edge
and fall away, waterfall of shattered droplets.
                                Instead I circle the sea,
        asteroid in orbit, no hope
                        to be released.

I mark time not by moon,
        but stars I've seen vanish
                since I began to drift.
        Lights that lived a million years
                        have burned out in my lifetime.
        Ursa Major, Great Bear,
                skinned of her luminous fur.
Orion reduced to shoulder and hip.

                Only Draco remains complete:
        wings, skull, and backbone
stretching the night. Above my head,
        heaven collapses, star by star. I wait and watch
                as the world distills to water, salt,
                        wind, darkness, dragon,
                                and me.

A Week's Pay
LOST AT THE
Lizard Fight

WITHIN THE BIRD STORM

I couldn't explain how one day at dusk
ten million wings began beating around my head,

the feathers and cawing weaving a cyclone,
how I had become the eye of the bird storm.

The wind they created tangled my hair
into branches of brambles, and I planted my feet,

refusing to be sucked into migration. Days later,
I felt a lump swell in my chest and, fearing the worst,

squeezed with my fingers until the shell cracked,
and felt through my torso the cold drip of yolk.

I coughed up pinfeathers and hollow bones,
which I cleaned and assembled into our family

tree, but I lacked enough links to draw evolution
from bird into man. Inside me, egg after egg calcified,

the secrets of flight trapped in my lungs.
At last, a speckled shell emerged intact from my throat,

blue as the sky for which it was destined.
But the thing hatched wingless. Stumbling about

on needle-thin legs, it bled a steady trickle
from a hole in its brain.

Like the walls of the bird storm, I formed a nest
for the hatchling within my cupped palms.

Spring still arrives every year of my life,
but I've stopped waiting for the flock to return.

THE EPA WARNS AGAINST CONSUMPTION OF ANGEL MEAT

*I*t used to be you could get whole slabs for less
than lamb per pound. Refrigerated warehouses
would dangle the day's catch over grates to let
the glitter run, and halos would be ground up
for dental fillings and costume jewelry. The fields
the weeks before Good Friday—whitewashed
with their folded wings—would glow all evening:
so many angels we couldn't sleep for their luminosity.
Grandpa would explain how their flesh was veined
with sunlight; the meat had to drain awhile
or else it was just like biting a star. But now,
you find them washed up dead in creeks,
blight corroding their petal-soft skin, and tests
of blood and feathers show their bodies carry
more mercury than water. Eating one today
is like swallowing a spoonful of melted silver.
It stains the tongue and teeth.

A Week's Pay Lost
at the Lizard Fight

*Y*ou drop your roll of Friday bills
on the purple one with a thick black
tongue, because its yellow eyes
haven't shifted from its opponent,
a green skink clawing the walls
of the box, cold-footed gladiator
wetting its corner.
But when the fight ends
with your pick split open,
neck to rectum, organs spilt
like pink confetti, you'll wander home,
thinking of how to win it all back.

Even at six you'd ask your dad
what could kill what: Great white or gorilla?
Cobra or buffalo? Neanderthal or
Green Beret? Everything eyed
in potential death matches. Every day
you find yourself standing across
another new monster eager to empty
your torso. You'll get lost, circle the city,
forget your way home as you dream
of a box big enough to fit
you in one corner
and the entire world in the other.

CATERPILLARS

When we were little, we'd delight
in the season of caterpillars. They'd crawl
on the trees, and we'd scoop up a couple
to wriggle in our palms or tickle our legs.

When I moved away, I learned most people
call them leeches, but where I was born
we had so few words, everything had to share
a name or went its existence unmentioned.

For example, wolf could mean *pet*,
but also *mother* or *rusted machine* or
tree where tired angels rest.

When I first moved, believe me,
there were lots of misunderstandings.
I'd just point to things constantly,
That's *what I mean! You call it* what?

A gaggle of caterpillars could nuzzle
a dead wolf down to bone in a few hours.
That was great joy and relief, especially
if the wolf belonged to one of us.

Where I was born, love meant *blind,
the tea that soothes stomach ulcers,* or
anything you felt all the way to your pinky toes.

I've been away a long time from where
I was born, but every now and then I
still make mistakes. I'll reminisce and share
a memory like *the troll we loved to rub
as kids in the woods.*

And when I get blank stares, I just say,
"Oh, I guess you had to be there," which I've learned
in my new home means *connection lost, reboot* or
I've given up on trying or
you will never know the real me.

ORIGINS OF THE
LIZARD MAN

*Y*ou were conceived beneath a cluster of stars
called *Cannibal*, named by your ancestors who saw
great swaths of sky

swallowed by light. A constellation of white needle teeth
that snapped at chunks of helpless darkness.
Be grateful you don't

remember the den of your mother's womb,
a nine-month captivity entangled with a dozen
others just like you,

slick scrum of thoughtless reptiles. You writhed
and chewed each other's tails, knowing there'd be
enough milk

for only one in this world.
And you were so goddamn thirsty even then.
You bit and bit

noses, toes, still-soft bones until the sea of her belly
was a morgue for your weaker brothers. Who could blame you?
When you were born,

you opened your fist, pink finger
by finger, and tested your grip like the bite of a lizard
on your mother's breast,

leaving purple lilacs on her skin, a garland of bruises.
You learned from the stars to keep your nerves packed—
patient and tight—

prepared for any moment to burst. Before your first sunrise,
you already knew the cold blooded of the earth never
close their eyes.

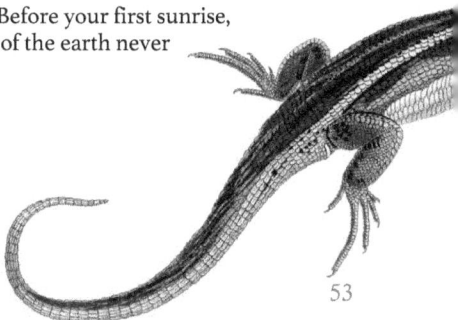

IN THE DUNKIN' DONUTS WHERE THE VIRGIN MARY APPEARED ON AN APPLE FRITTER

E very day since that report,
    I've ordered a fritter
        and sat by the window

        to inspect its frosting
    for Teresa's laugh lines,
        Jesus' beard,

anything to prove
    there's more for me today

    than coffee and subways
and a burned-out porchlight
    I've yet to fix.

God didn't have to make it so hard,
        you know,
    if He wanted me to believe.

He didn't have to let
    miracles run dry
        in my century.

        Another weekday.
Another secular fritter.
    From the window,

    I see a boy chase
a lost ball into a bush.
    Thank God it's not burning.

The Northernmost Edge
of the
Star-Wasting Syndrome

E ve, what's left to envy? The sky's so old and petty now.

Take your rest unguarded.

No devils will bother to gremlin your dreams any longer.

If Celestials still demand blame, I'll furnish the scarecrows with spears
to guard your last harvest.

Defiance—iron-tipped weapon aimed at the bruised shields
of an infested empire.

If you gave away what could have been, it all turned white, then cold,
regardless.

Rubbed raw by war the edges curled, the glut of the center collapsed.

All evidence shows they're dying out fast, imbalanced quaternion,
the fires no longer replenished.

Mother, thank you for these last two stars: One I'll eat now while it's still
blood-red and fresh.

The other I'll watch behind glass as it shrinks. White dwarf, sacred,
the size of a fist.

No one could blame us for keeping this one to ourselves.

ANTON LAVEY'S BLAZER

I own a blazer that once belonged
to his Satanic Majesty, Anton LaVey.
The lining is shredded. Two buttons gone.

Even so, a thrift-shop steal. Five bucks bought me
a gabardine coat and his ghost who lists about
my apartment, translucent, the tired smoke
of a long burned-out fire.

In the left inner pocket, I uncovered a lock
of hair that sheltered his heart till the last
of his Earth days, all he had left of his beloved,
Jayne Mansfield. Each strand of near-white blond
is tie-dyed pink by the blood of her gushing carotid.

In '67, his hex was a thumb at her neck
and when she refused him, he snapped off
her dandelion head and carried
that mistake like a cairn of flat stones
in his stomach.

Sometimes while shaving, I see in the mirror
him cradle her headless body, humming
Vivaldi, which few knew she loved.

Chilly mornings, I'll wear his blazer and scan
AM radio for the classical station. Not that I'm
a fan. I just know that sometimes even the devil longs
to shake the ice that crusts his wings and tongue,
to talk to God once more and teach Him
the meaning of the words *regret* and *forgiveness*.

STANDING NAKED IN THE FOREST AT THE HEIGHT OF MOSQUITO SEASON

*S*houlder to wrist, this arm
        is yours. I will not swat
            the tender divide between
bicep and tricep, or
      the soft, hairless pocket
           of the elbow's crook.
      Needle your mouth
           for a sip, and delight
in blood's salty warmth
           as it flushes your cavities
      like a long pull of brandy.
                Let your shell shimmer
      with iron-laced heat.

Call the others: The six-legged,
      the eight-, the hundred-,
           the thousand-. The mandibles,
             proboscides, the spikes
and wings. The ones that sting,
            the ones that poison,
      the ones that harbor
    infectious diseases, the ones
that lay eggs in intimate
             hollows. From neck to crotch,
      this is yours. I will not flinch
        as my skin swells out,
    a bloated scarlet. I will not scream or curse
        your name to God.
             I don't blame you for your thirst.
        We all take, you know.
We've all drunk someone dry.

DIRT EATERS ANONYMOUS

*S*tare at her hands during dinner.
Dirt under the nails
is a sure sign of relapse. Ask,
"Honey, how was your day?
Did you garden?"
Watch her blush and squeak
out a lie, so little air   able to wheeze through her throat;
her pinhole windpipe   dammed back with black loam.

Kiss her in bed and taste   bitter topsoil,
her lips cracked from leaves   that suck
the skin's moisture,   leaving her brittle
like yellowing edges   of autumn.
Run your tongue
over her teeth and   cut yourself
on the twigs stuck between.

Don't fall asleep.   Wait till she slips
from under your arm,   slips out the bedroom,
slips into darkness,   strips off her clothes
and rolls in the grass,   the bed of gardenias,
munching on mulch till she's foaming,
delirious.

Don't call the doctor.   It's not her fault.
Maybe you thought since you'd   been inside her

it was you she was missing,
the way you fit   seemed a circuit completed.
You began to believe your
presence belonged in all her hollow spaces.

You forgot   before she was yours   she was miles of elements pleated,
sand and clay,   wood and silt,
an unbroken chain of molecules hooked
like a harness to the earth that begot her.

The pebbles know her longing.

Let her fill the empty spaces.
Let her find her way back home.

THE GOSPEL ACCORDING TO HOMO HABILIS

*I*n the beginning there was Tree, and we fell from Tree and were Its children, for we, too, stood with heads like branches to the sky.

²Tree begot flowers and It dropped the Fruit whose seven seeds bloomed into the Seven Heads of God.

³We breathe and each breath is a prayer to all the Names of the Lord, because They were born of the same Fruit:

⁴God the Eye Open, who bleeds His own light for our warmth. We feed under His sky.

⁵God the Eye Closed, who turns away His face. He lets the wolves circle and scream our names at night.

⁶God the Fanged Tiger, who leaves the killing fresh and offers us the sacrifice before the crows descend.

⁷God the Stone, both the Thin that cuts the flesh apart and the Heavy that crushes bone so we may suck the sweet mud within.

⁸God the One Like Us But Swifter, who steals our fruit and comes closer and closer each day.

⁹God the Water, from whose belly we sip as it slides along the grass, always giving, always enough.

¹⁰God the Mastodon, whose name is carved on glaciers and sounds the same as *fear*.

¹¹So it has been, the children of the Tree still falling and grasping what passes by in our hands.

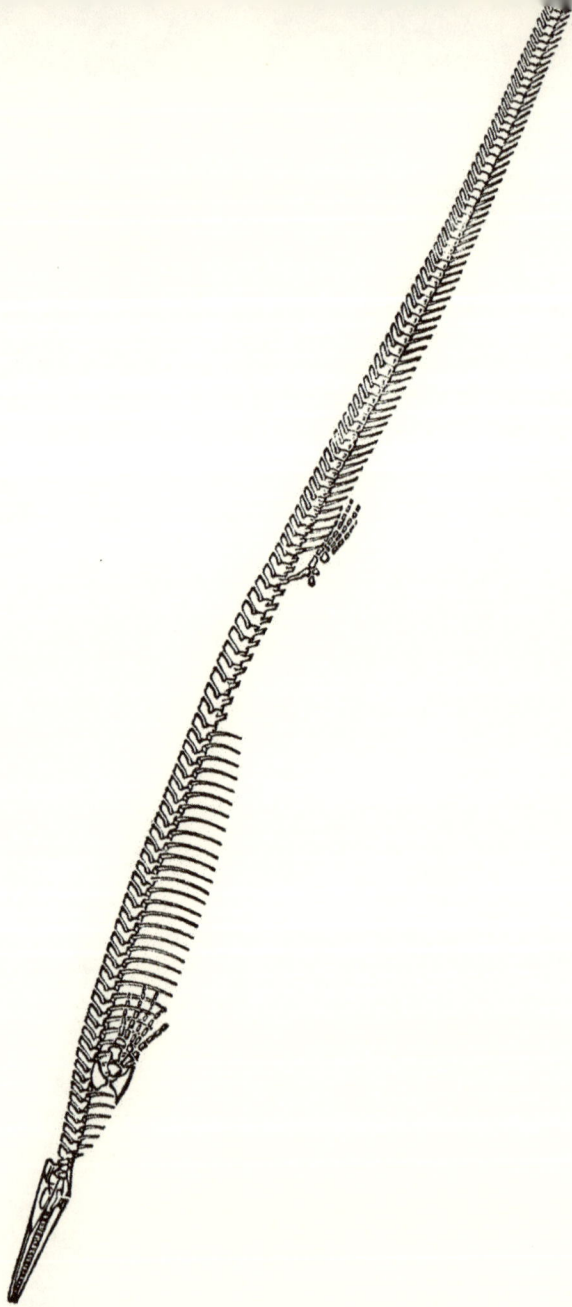

"Fickle their state whom God most favors!
Who can please Him long?
Me first He ruined, now mankind.
Who will He next?"

—*Satan in John Milton's* Paradise Lost, *Book VIII*

The Hard HAND OF Cataclysm

"Some say a comet will fall from the sky.
Followed by meteor showers and tidal waves.
Followed by fault lines that cannot sit still.
Followed by millions of dumbfounded dipshits."

—*Tool, "Aenema"*

In Mission, Kansas, on the Brink of the Latest Apocalypse

*C*an You forgive us tonight, one last time,
for our dumb mutton habits as we while
our final hours of this snake-bit Creation,
same as our race has for two thousand centuries:
coveting our neighbor's slippers and bandsaw,
working a graveyard shift on the Sabbath.

At QuikTrip Gas, off I-35, a dropout
stuffs strawberry Pop-Tarts and Kotex
in her hoodie's deep lair below
her thieving heart. Can she, too, be forgiven?
Or the cashier who sees
and just doesn't care, and sullies Your name
every time the Chiefs play? How about the truck drivers
trading amphetamines, and astronomers
on NPR mocking the End Times
who claim with their prying, impertinent
telescopes, that if You built the sky,
it was a slapdash operation beyond
Your control, that sinkholes of black gravity
corrode, as rust does, the edges of everything
You made.

Can I be forgiven for filling my tank as if
I still had 400 miles of road in my lifetime?
Forgive my not knowing the Act of Contrition
anymore, for wasting my last wish
on molasses-smoked brisket rather than
salvation? Forgive, God, my glee,
as I drive toward the widest horizon
I've seen, dawn like the drawbridge
of the devil's jaw. Forgive my not stopping
as morning unhinges
my anticipation for burning stone,
for ample fire.

"Fear not
for I am with thee,"

Says the One whose pouch is packed with asteroids
and Whose fingers, licked, can pinch out the sun,
Who strikes dead your firstborn and sheep when annoyed
with His saltshaker of locusts and asteroids.
Fear not, but know, He began with a void
and since the first Sabbath has mourned what He'd done.
He watches while thumbing His worry stone asteroids
etched with the names of your daughters and sons.

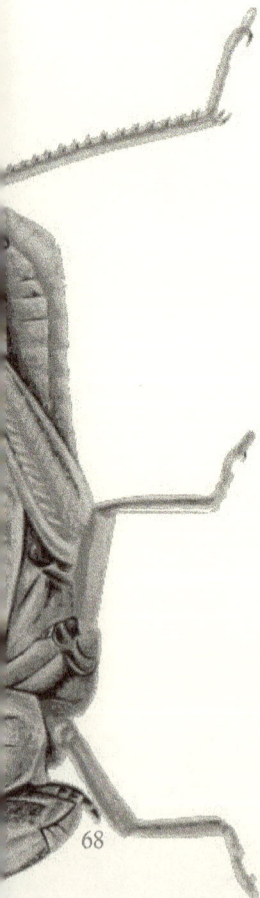

A Refugee
of the Bone Wars

*I*t's a nervy gambit, a thousand upfront
for fare across the Boreal Sea,
humid days of steamed-milk air,
plesiosaurs nipping the ferryman's oars.
Three days until land, then the balance paid
on the muddy banks of the Mesozoic.
Moldy bushmeat, a knowledge of mushrooms.
That's all the ferryman has to offer,
plus a prayer for safe passage that neither of us
holds faith in.

> If God is good and made us
> in His image, then all men are carpenters,
> sawing and sanding, and later resenting how
> nothing turns out the way we imagined.

I'm done with the Bone Wars,
deep in the marl pits where we'd pile the mule carts
with all of God's failures discarded in limestone.
And what of it, a payday for skulls
if my own rests snug in the Winchester crosshairs
of a Marsh or Cope goon high on the ridge,
thumbing the hammer?
It takes no tealeaves to divine our die-off,
the furless mammals of Como Bluffs,
feeding on gold, blind to the asteroids.

> If Neanderthal roots our family tree,
> then we are each children with hands
> of the spear-maker. We still have not fashioned
> a weapon so fearsome it repels the will of the Lord.

No longer for fortune, I prospect only a soft place
to hide. I bushwhacked cycads, macheted dragonflies
wide as owls to build here my shelter.
A sauropod palace, scarf-jointed femurs,
archways of vertebrae; I'm the lone working organ
inside this dead beast. I'll ride out the reckoning
as refugees do, bargaining every drop of blood I can spare
for enough to wager tomorrow.

If Eden was sowed on forsaken soil
of a scorched first Creation, then we must uncover
the book before Genesis and brace ourselves for its ending.
So many creatures once shaped by His hands
now erased. And of all His children,
He must regret us most.

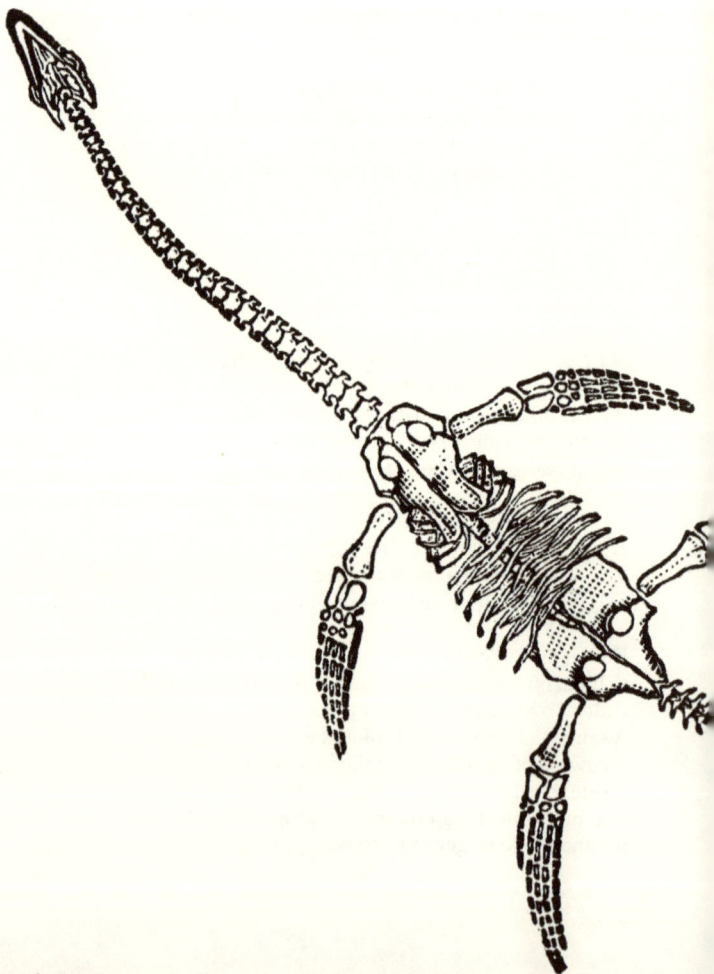

GAMBLER'S RUIN, BLUE STAG CASINO

This stretch of highway stinks with shit
of industrial pig farms, is lit only
by a series of billboards for the Blue Stag Casino,
Home of the World's Finest Prime Rib Buffet.

For weeks now radio waves have been bashing
the prairies with prophecies, threats of Apocalypse,
and the devout—or bet hedgers—
have erected makeshift calvaries
from scrap wood and shovel handles.
Like lambs' blood smeared
on their town welcome signs, it's their plea
to the Lord, *We beseech You,*
command Your angels to hold still their scythes
as they pass this unincorporated community.

God, I'm not marking myself for Passover.
I just want to know the odds of this game.
Do my chances increase in the Blue Stag Casino,
less loathsome by proxy in a House of Smoke
where the chips are blessed like communion wafers?

What are the odds for the pensioned elderly,
the nicotine addicts, the children of genocide
dumping the ashtrays, dealing a straight?

When the clock winds to zero, whose souls
will You choose to touch with Your blessing,
leaving a rumple of clothes on the floor still sweaty
and hot from the miracle?

I'm only here to stretch my legs, fill my mug
with complimentary coffee, a gamble that saving
two dollars on gas station brew will matter at all
tomorrow. How much we each wager tonight
depends on what we believe. If this is it,
we've everything to lose.

When we lay our bets down in the House of the Lord,
God, we forget Your limitless bank, galaxies down
to the spiral staircase of our own DNA, everything Yours,
even our trembling fingers, trying our best to hide from You
our hand.

FIELD OF BULLETS,
MEDICINE BOW

*F*orty-five dollars of regular unleaded.
 My gas tank is a graveyard on fire.
Most every species that once drew breath
is fossil now, or oil. If I'm to die
in this latest Apocalypse, what would my body
ignite? Whose escape could I fuel?

Wyoming, too, is an unmarked grave
and the wind shears off an inch
each year to flash the bones of another
failure felled by the hard hand of cataclysm.
All my escape routes are paved
on the backs of a billion extinctions.

As the Cretaceous closed,
did You gather Your children
in a field to graze while You scooped
in Your two open palms the width
of continents a handful of celestial stones
to scatter like snowflakes upon their gaping
mouths?

Or did You close one eye
and aim?

"HE THAT IS WITHOUT SIN AMONG YOU, LET HIM FIRST CAST A STONE."

—John 8:7

*H*e sighs and steps forward: the only one.

He kneels and packs the dirty snow
into a comet. His hands grow numb

with the ache of always being the only one.
He folds in stars and iridium

so dense He's certain with just one blow
He'll leave Creation barren. No one

left praying as the crater fills with snow.

A Reading from the Book of Modern Extinctions

> "Are not two sparrows sold for a penny?
> Yet not one of them will fall to the ground
> outside your Father's care."
> —Matthew 10:29

The fields were barely dried of blood in August 1864,
when the soil turned over to the season of autumn,
then for us, the season of without,
war orphans, hairless, skilled only in marching
two steps behind our stone-pit starvation,
feral with hunger.

Then spring brought the season of passenger
pigeons, a Nor'easter of wings frothing the air.
Three billion birds, lust-drugged and mindless,
a deafening cloud wide as all the Alleghenies.
The sky congealed with preening stink and darkness.

·

A week of work with Reverend Camping,
eighty boys like me, eager for a mule's job.
Shotguns, buckshot, sacks of sulfur
strapped across our bone-ridged backs.
Cheaper, too, with nimble fingers
small enough to pluck a dove
clean to goosebump skin
in less than half a minute.

Fourteen hours we trudged beneath
the shadow of that flock, the weather of April
a daylong sleet of shit that bleached our hats
gray-white. A lame-legged boy, lagging behind,
tried to curry Reverend's favor, shouldered
his shotgun and, without aiming, dropped fifty
birds like hail upon our heads.

The Reverend's fist burst the cripple's face
louder than the gun blast. The boy squirmed
in mud amongst the scattered bird parts.
*Don't waste buckshot. When our Lord cleaned
the House of the Pharaoh, He waited until Passover.
We'll take what the Lord has promised us if we
prove our patience.*

The boy tried to keep up as we hastened the march,
but grew smaller and smaller behind us
until he was no longer.

•

Our caravan camped where the flock had nested,
glazing the forests with fluttering blue.
The woods were steeped in their mating.

Still, we didn't pull a trigger. We waited
for the eggs to hatch, for squabs to plump
and bend the boughs. Nightlong vigils,
we guarded our garden of birds, guns perched for poachers
eying the nests, their empty nets left wanting.

Reverend knew the hour had come
when the first dove lifted from the oaks,
breaking the canopy and the spell of the nesting season.
We boys spread sulfur below each tree and lit
the yellow sand on fire. Covered our mouths
with carbon-soaked wool, but still could taste
the acrid smoke blister open our lips.

The Tenth Plague on the House of Pennsylvania:
the glowing stink of the forest and the blizzard
of falling birds, stomachs melted by fumes.

•

Reverend made us pray before he doled to each his wages,
a postage stamp and a sackful of birds.
Even waifs like you, the Lord does not forget.
His ledger counts each hair you've grown and shed today
and always. The House of God is full to bursting,
unending for His faithful. Nothing happens without His blessings.

If God were watching what we did in the woods,
He didn't blink. If God knew the number
of feathers stitched upon each fallen body,
He counted, as well, the sulfur grains burned.
If a sparrow could not fall outside His care,
He did not care enough even to save their bones.

"... A WISE MAN'S HEART DISCERNETH BOTH TIME AND JUDGMENT."

—*Ecclesiastes 8:5*

*I*t's super attuned and beats to the kill clock, minus or plus
an hour, but close enough to know *Sell the house and repent.*
Its alarm flashes *Apocalypse* in red. The Lord Almighty is just,
His message clear, and the wise man's heart can tell (minus or plus
a day) eclipses and earthquakes are near; it must
buy billboard space and warn the less discerning. His heart laments
those dumber hearts—functional but void of faith—that cannot tell, plus
or minus this lifetime, that shit's going down. *Kneel, fool. Repent.*

Simple Math, Sweet Grass County

"Five times 10 times 17
is telling you a story."
—Reverend Harold Camping

H is prophecy champed the bit too hard.
Three days delayed, or so I'm guessing. Who knows?
All dawn, lightning's crooked fingers have jabbed
the Cayuse Hills to purple, fried to cracklin'
what few local stations my radio catches
in Sweet Grass County, Montana.

Or, perhaps, this really is
the last my species has to say.
An epilogue of static, postscript as the world
splits open a crack in Earth's mantle long as I-90,
exposing the planet's magma-red bloodline.

With two residents per square mile,
if any had been raptured how would I even notice?
No cars abandoned. Travelers like me don't earn
salvation if we won't even deign to park and remove
our flip-flops on this highest of holy days.

I'm just making such good time. It's simple math:
twenty over the generous speed limit, plus tailwind.
A hubris in thinking no troopers or horsemen are following.
His math? A story told in numbers:

Five for atonement, my fingers that brush
the beads of the rosary hung from the rearview,
those sorrowful mysteries braided in wax.

Ten for completeness, the toes to walk the path
of the Lord. Adam to Noah: ten generations of our species
allowed our missteps, our fuck-ups until God, fed up,
releases the Flood.

Seventeen, for Heaven. My number of road hours
from Kansas, Wyoming, into southern Montana.
God's Country, the closest to Heaven I'll get.

And God, what math are You solving today?
Is this planet a bead on Your abacus? Do You
slide and slide us to subtract, pushing apart
the wheat and the chaff? Bundle the saved.
Turn Your back from the rest in the burning field.

"FOR HE SHALL GIVE HIS ANGELS CHARGE OVER YOU AND KEEP YOU IN ALL YOUR WAYS,"

—Psalm 91:11

So when the Devil dares you to climb the Chrysler Building and jump,
His angels are stationed—imperial force—armored and ready
to catch you. Shucks, should you even trip on a cobblestone bump,
they'll bear you up; they stand at attention until He says, "Jump!"
And if it be His will to raze Manhattan to stumps,
they'll hoist their axes in phalanx, hold steady.
From the borders of Heaven, they're waiting to jump
onto Sodom, Pangea, wherever. Armed. Spring-loaded. They're ready.

THE SECOND PASS
OF THE SCYTHE

I never see the ferryman come, but find the bottles he leaves
on the beach stuffed with the *New York Journal* so I may read
the world. There's war bursting open the seams of the globe;
I'm waiting my turn to fall in the fault lines. If he's ferried survivors,
I've never seen them. Footprints are swallowed by the black suck
of mudflats. Refugees vanish in the maw of the jungle.

> *Preparing for the final blow at Cuba.*
> The rain and the Lord are different here,
> heavier both. Daily they bless me
> whether I worship or not.

When flocks of Pteranodons are grounded by wind shears, I strip
their wings for roofing. Gingko bark braids make durable snares
to snap the necks of Compsognathus that run like pheasants, their flesh
when smoked a firmer trout. Rock pools gather the springwells and rain.
My stomach now knows this country's particulars
and doesn't turn from a bite of raw fruit.

> *125,000 Volunteers Are Assigned to War Stations.*
> I've stowed away on the Ark of Extinction.
> A lost battalion, colossal beasts deployed
> to the warfront of amnesia.

I, too, am a species cast out from Ohio; primitive hominid, a bloodline
fetid with scavengers, snakes. After the War, pulled chickens from farms
and harvested pigeons by millions. Plundered crypts, dug bones, grabbed
at whatever the Gold Hoarders wanted dearly enough to pinch off a bit
from their pots for me. Anything short of shooting a man
to sell his still-fresh heart.

> *Awful Slaughter—Our Troops at Manila Killed Filipinos by the Thousands.*
> God knows every inch of His world,
> but the cartographers are closing in
> drawing the borders the predators haunt.

Every species is the Chosen One until God's gaze turns cold.
The world still has pockets to hide but fewer and fewer each day.
Does the Angel that loosed the Tenth Plague on Pharaoh
return the way he came? Does he double-back, swinging
the scythe of his touch to cut down the stalks he missed at first pass?
Does he answer to *Olympia* now? To *Warship*? To *Ironsided Wings*?

"AND HE AROSE, AND REBUKED THE WIND, AND SAID UNTO THE SEA, PEACE, BE STILL."

—*Mark 4:39*

At last calm blue. He hushed and cleansed the sea.
The reckless wild He stilled to precious stones.
The ammonites destroyed. Menageries
of quartz and hollow shells adorn the sea.
Disgusted by their tentacles and teeth,
His sickle fingers scythed the overgrown.
Mistakes repaired, it pleases Him to see
their flesh dissolved. Just lifeless shells made stone.

Complex Math, Teton County

*M*ontana dusk is pyrite is grain dust is heat.

This haze fools my eyes to believe I can catch
the Earth's edge with just a bit more speed.
No rest and this drive smears the mileposts into
the white-petal chokecherries that flank my exodus.

If the planet's curve can be approximated
by straight lines that mimic the arcs,
how fast must I go to flatten the Earth?

I can't help but dare my car to test this geometry.

Two millennia past, the circle obsessed Archimedes,
driven to unravel pi, celestial number whose digits extend
onward to the ceiling of Heaven. His math like
my car cutting nearer still to the unknowable.

First approximation: Hexagon. Six sides
for the imperfection of man.

Second approximation: Dodecagon. Twelve
stars in the crown of a mother whose womb
is the fertile soil of endless war.

Final approximation: a shape so close to circle
it has no better name. But the old mathematician never tried
to draw the 96 lines that edged closer and closer to the divine.
The horizon of his knowing: still just his best guess.

My speedometer bends so deep into red
it can finish its circle if I trespass the impossible,
overtake the sunset. But another horizon still haunts me:
the K-T boundary, a snake of spacedust uncoiled
through all the canyons, iridescent scales of fireball ejecta.
A reminder—quiet as a reptile digesting—of what You
are willing to do to us when provoked to wrath.

And I, like Babel, reckless and trespassing, must make
Your fingers itch to grab the nearest stone
to strike down my hands, sew my lips silent
with the thread of silver iridium.

GROWING OLD IN THE RIBCAGE OF EXTINCTION

> "He shall cover you with his feathers,
> and under his wings
> you shall take refuge."
> —Psalm 91:4

March 1941

And these are the twelve tribes of therapod:
Tyrannosaurus, Ceratosaurus, Valkerie, Whiptail.
Gargoyle, Blue Adder, Gharial Toad.
Egg Thief, Bug Hunter. Sickle-Toed Thing
That Wails Like a Woman. Mouth of One Hundred
Pike Bayonets. The last, no name but Devil.

Today starts the season their feathers shed
bearing lust plumage beneath. Molt chokes
the air; my lungs are all torn by this gray hazy punk.
Barb-tipped filaments, like sulfur on fire,
like volcanic ash.

•

July 1941

Moses, did Midianites haunt you like pigeons do my dreams of late?
Did their ghosts mop your brow as you died at the door of God's
        promise?

•

February 1942

Long ago, the bottles stopped coming. I don't know
what it means, but I've spent a score searching
for answers while my knees rotted through,
while my teeth fell like snow.

On the hillside I chiseled a stone for the ferryman,
filled a grave with ammonite shells. But rain and seeds
infest the inscription. Roots take hold and break his name.

•

November 1943

Noah, I'm lost. The doves of my life have all been shot down. The ravens
       have left me forsaken.
Your refugee blood courses thickly within me, but slower one pulse beat
       each day.

•

June 1944

The Dry Season breaks when monsoons make landfall,
but this year the weather is a gathering stormfront
of bullets. Pteranodons crash with tattered wings
like autumn mallards shredded by buckshot. What manner of being
is manning these guns? How keen is his sight? Does he see me
hold my breath as he passes, strafing the moon?

My refuge, the hull of Leviathan. When will be my turn,
slayed and hollowed for sanctuary to shelter what God
chooses next for His mercy? The angels have charge—
a thousand on either side fall—but the walls of the storm
are collapsing, shrinking the eye.

•

October 1944

Jesus, you hungered in wilderness with only the Devil to talk to.
Angels wait for me at the foot of the hill, but they won't show
       their hands. They never smile.

December 1945

In the last bottle the ferryman left me, I collected
my cracked teeth. Because I never took a wife,
because I haven't a son to bequeath
what I saved, I left it at the shore to be taken by tide.
Each a precious stone I had to pay to survive extinction,
a lifetime of war.

On the final day, I'll journey once more to the shore and lie
in the delta, wrapped in mud, a richer shroud than silk.
Whatever walks this world next can unearth my bones,
arrange my ribs, place a penny where my heart would have rested,
and guess the name of the god I prayed to before my throat
was filled—as with grace or penance—with silt.

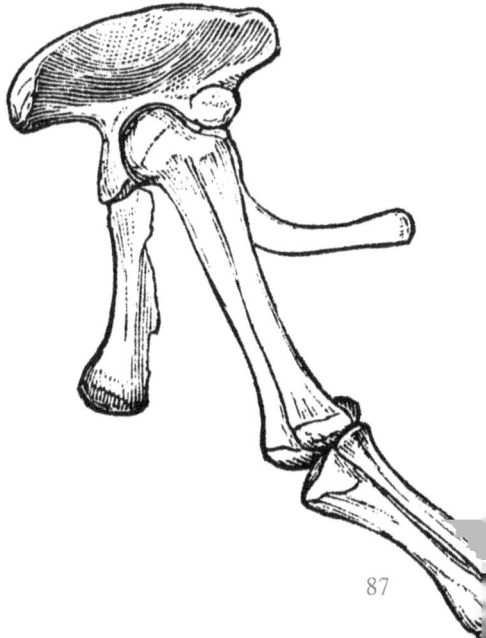

Minimum Viable Population, Cape Alava

I'm out of road. Terra firma, but barely,
and the spit I stand on juts into the churning ocean,
defiant chin of a wobbled boxer who's got
no chance to last the round.

This isn't the water that soothes the sick,
not water that smooths out blankets of silt
to cradle our dead and gently remove
our feathers and eyes, leaving intact the bones
made beautiful with copper and quartz,
loved enough to save.

Were I to die before the Pacific, my scapula, femur,
the jewelry box of my ribcage,
would be pounded to powder by surf.

This ocean bites the cliff apart.
Battered pines defy the wind, cling
by root hairs. Still
they persist. It doesn't take much. Just a sliver
of daylight, I guess.

Same then for us, bloodline of a chosen species.
Whether or not we're still Your chosen,
we still are holding on.

Imagine then, me Isaac, my father's hands
trembling with age and heartache,
binding me, a crying boy in vines,
cooing in my ear, *Hush, hush my beloved.*

But at that moment his whetted blade
prepares to honor Your blessings
by dipping into my pink-flushed throat,
the angel this time lands late,
delayed in the stars.

Even then, after all my wasted blood
there sits patient Ishmael. He would have been
enough.

So I haven't been running from You.
If the saved have been lifted
into the corona of Your warmth
the rest of us survived in the dark, grew wild.
If the first strike of the Apocalypse
never comes, Doomsday has been
building every day of our lives, each of us a domino
just waiting our turn to topple.

If Your will is the wave that takes and takes
with grinding force our footing on this world,
then may Your grace be the new moon,
dark hole of Your mouth
peeling back the water to reveal
what we were always meant to be:
the limitless sand, wet, unsteady,
but stable enough for whoever
tends this planet next to stand.

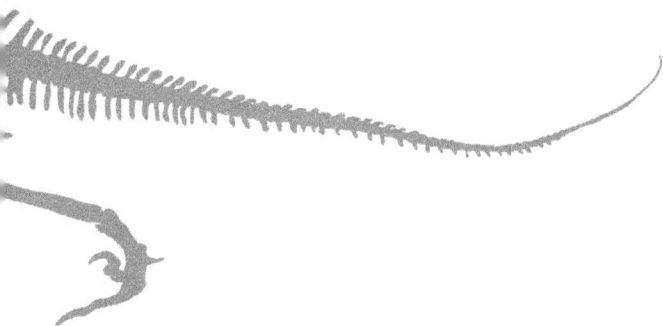

"UNTO ADAM ALSO AND TO HIS WIFE DID THE LORD GOD MAKE COATS OF SKINS, AND CLOTHED THEM."

—*Genesis 3:21*

Because He locked the Garden. Because Outside
was Glacier, and their skin till then had known no cold.
Because He watched Blue Northers lash their cheeks and eyes
as they stumbled barefoot on snow outside,
He plucked the mastodon and snapped its spine, peeled back the hide
to sew for them a little warmth. His children survived, grew old,
thanks to this sacrifice. Because sending them Outside
cracked wide His heart. Because He'd kill to save them from the cold.

ABOUT THE AUTHOR

Armin Tolentino

grew up in New Jersey and received his MFA at Rutgers University in Newark. His poetry has appeared in *Hyphen Magazine, Arsenic Lobster, The Raven Chronicles,* and elsewhere. He lives in Vancouver, Washington, with his wife and her three chinchillas.

Author Notes
on the Text

The epigraph for "Suspended Memories" comes from the song "Space Oddity" by David Bowie.

The "Bone Wars" refers to a period of time between 1877 and 1892, when the two paleontologists Edward Drinker Cope and Othniel Charles Marsh competed bitterly for the discovery of new fossils in the American West. Their feud led to the identification of over 100 species of dinosaurs in North America and increased the public's awareness of creatures that lived long before human existence, a realization that must have been ground-shattering for people who believed entirely in the story of Creation.

Gambler's Ruin is a popular hypothetical problem in statistics that states, perhaps contrary to our general hunch, a fifty-fifty bet will lead assuredly to bankruptcy for the party that starts with less (e.g. gambler versus the house). Statistical paleontologist David M. Raup uses this model to describe the near certainty for the extinction of every species that has ever lived: "Eventual extinction of the genus is assured. This is somewhat counterintuitive, but it follows from the presence of the single absorbing boundary at zero species. If there is no upper absorbing boundary, the random walk is bound to hit the lower boundary eventually." It's impossible for a genus to keep evolving infinitely into new species, so instead, it will die out when enough time passes.

The Field of Bullets hypothesis describes a model in which extinction is non-selective and occurs randomly. The metaphor suggests that species are simply out in a field, and "bullets" are hitting them at random, thus their extinction operates without relation to their adaptability.

"... a wise man's heart discerneth both time and judgment," was one of the Bible quotes found on Radio One billboards throughout the nation in May 2011.

The late Reverend Harold Camping of Family Radio predicted the world would end on May 21, 2011, based on math he calculated from the Bible. In an interview, he said, "Five times 10 times 17 is telling you a story."

Italicized lines in "The Second Pass of the Scythe" are headlines from the *New York Journal* during the Spanish/American and Philippine/American Wars.

Minimum Viable Population describes the lower boundary of a species' numbers necessary for it to survive in the wild. The smaller the population, the more susceptible it is to extinction; however, populations can last a remarkably long time despite low numbers. For instance, the Laysan Duck, native to Hawaii, was once believed to have only seven adults and five juveniles in its population in 1912, but it somehow persists today.

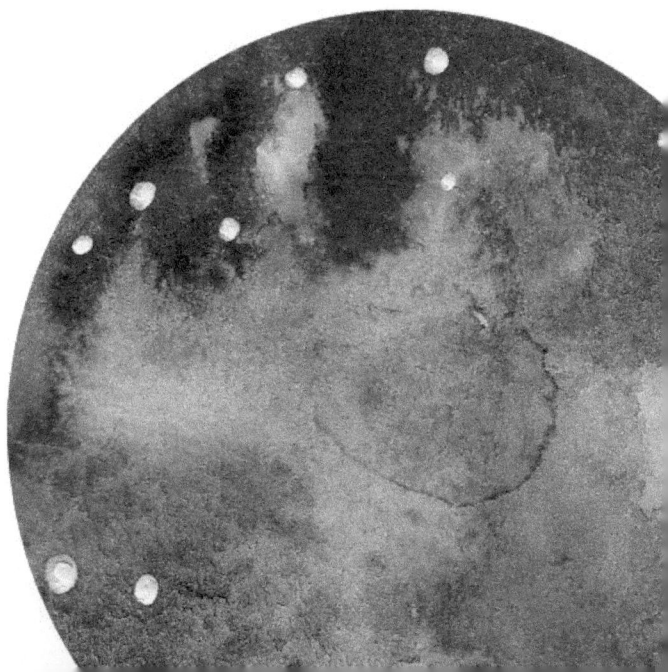

Author Thanks

Many poems in this collection were inspired by the writings of statistical paleontologist David M. Raup, specifically his book *Extinction: Bad Genes or Bad Luck?* We were never the first on this planet, and we likely will not be the last.

To the tireless folks at Alternating Current Press—thank you for seeing something in the rubble of a manuscript and polishing it to a shine.

Forever grateful to the faculty and students at Rutgers Newark for giving me a chance to learn and grow, as a writer and as a man.

Much love to the Third Tuesday Poets in Portland for your encouragement and your astute eyes, often the first to look at these poems.

My deepest appreciation to Literary Arts for the C. Hamilton Bailey Oregon Literary Fellowship and for welcoming me into the community—you remind us all that we don't do this work in isolation.

To Mama, Papa, Ate—nothing I do would be possible without you, and I never say that enough.

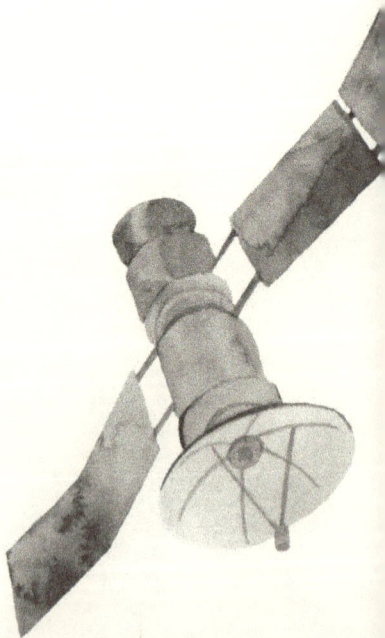

ACKNOWLEDGMENTS

"Spaceboy's First Mission, Age Twelve (boat launch)," "A Letter That Spaceboy Never Received (blastoff)," "Spaceboy's Wife Builds a Widow's Walk," "Spaceboy Gives a Eulogy at His Mentor's Funeral," and "Stress Tests and Survival Skills" first appeared in *Night Music Journal*.

"Within the Bird Storm" and "Dirt Eaters Anonymous" first appeared in *South Mountain Writers Anthology*.

"The EPA Warns Against the Consumption of Angel Meat" first appeared in *Blue Earth Review*.

"A Week's Pay Lost at the Lizard Fight" and "Standing Naked in the Forest at the Height of Mosquito Season" first appeared in *Verseweavers*.

"Caterpillars" first appeared in *Arsenic Lobster*.

"Origins of the Lizard Man" first appeared in *Ellipsis*.

"In the Dunkin' Donuts Where the Virgin Mary Appeared on an Apple Fritter" first appeared in *Scintilla Magazine*.

"Anton LaVey's Blazer" first appeared in *Caravel Literary Arts Journal*.

"The Gospel According to *Homo Habilis*" first appeared in *Reservoir*.

"In Mission, Kansas, on the Brink of the Latest Apocalypse" and "A Refugee of the Bone Wars" first appeared in *The Bear Deluxe*.

"Gambler's Ruin, Blue Stag Casino," "Simple Math, Sweet Grass County," "Complex Math, Teton County," "Minimum Viable Population, Cape Alava," "'Fear not for I am with thee,'" "'He that is without sin among you, let him first cast a stone,'" "'For He shall give His angels charge over you and keep you in all your ways,'" and "'Unto Adam also and to his wife did the LORD God make coats of skins, and clothed them'" first appeared in *Common Knowledge*.

"Field of Bullets, Medicine Bow" first appeared in *New Millennium Writings*.

"The Second Pass of the Scythe" and "Growing Old in the Ribcage of Extinction" first appeared in *Rigorous*.

Colophon

The edition you are holding is the First Edition of this publication.

The cursive font used throughout the book is Katulamp, created by Resume Land. The capital letters of the cover and title pages is Dominican, and the interior title font is Dominican Small Caps, both created by Harold's Fonts. All secondary lettering and interior text is Athelas, created by José Scaglione and Veronika Burian. The Alternating Current Press logo is Portmanteau, created by JLH Fonts. All fonts are used with permission; all rights reserved.

The Alternating Current lightbulb logo was created by Leah Angstman, ©2013, 2019 Alternating Current. The whales were created by Everysunsun. The first sphere, rocket, second and third satellites, and meteorite were created by Marina Ermakova. The second sphere was created by Joanne Marie. The constellation maps are from *A Celestial Atlas* by Alexander Jamieson, first published in 1822, digitized courtesy of Digital Curio, and modified by Leah Angstman. The puff of smoke was created by Rudchenko. The lizards were created by Enliven Designs. The feathers and willow branch were created by Lovely Events Crafts. The first angel wing was created by Mete Humay. The dinosaur fossils are from an 1890 publication, digitized courtesy of Galapagos Field Co. The dinosaur skeleton silhouettes were created by Gluiki. The wheat and tentacles were created by Alfazet Chronicles. The second angel is titled "Why Peace Reigns," first published in *Puck Magazine* in 1898, digitized courtesy of Creation 7, and modified by Leah Angstman. The final sphere was created by Lana Elanor. Armin Tolentino's photo was taken by Michael G. England, ©2019. All other images were created by Leah Angstman or are in the public domain without attribution. Cover design by Leah Angstman. All graphics are used with permission; all rights reserved.

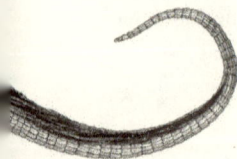

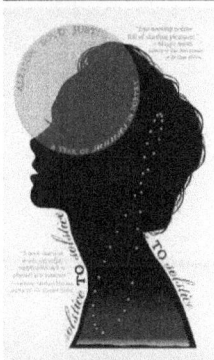

ALTERNATINGCURRENTARTS.COM